THE FIVE-GALLON BUCKET BOOK

105 Uses and Abuses for the Ultimate Recyclable

Jim McKenzie

W9-BIP-343

www.duluthtrading.com

99 00 01 02 03 SOL 10 9 8 7 6 5 4 3 2 1

Library of Congress Cataloging-in-Publication Data
McKenzie, Jim (Jim William)
    The five-gallon bucket book : 105 uses and abuses for the ultimate recyclable / by Jim McKenzie.
        p.   cm.
    ISBN 0-8362-8199-3 (pbk.)
    1. Plastics craft—Humor. 2. Pail—Recycling—Humor. I. Title.
TT297.M39 1999
745.5—dc21   98-50478
                                                                              CIP

All photographs by Wanda and Jim McKenzie.

THE FIVE-GALLON BUCKET BOOK

DEDICATION

For my very tolerant wife, Wanda, without whom this book would not have been possible.

To my daughters, Dianne and Susan, who I fear have inherited their father's sense of humor.

To my grandchildren, Allison, Daniel, and Dennis, who think it's *normal* to have a granddaddy who plays with plastic buckets.

To Max, who helped me carry the mirror, and Ted, who helped me fight the Giant.

Acknowledgments

A number of people, in one way or another, contributed to the completion of this book. I would like to take this opportunity to express my appreciation to them.

First, I would like to thank Kathleen and John Murdock for their generosity and patience in opening their home and computer to me when I was in a "spot."

I owe a debt of gratitude to my agent, Pat Snell, of the Michael Snell Literary Agency, for her insistence on the "perfect" proposal, and to her and Mike for the subsequent sale of it.

Thanks to Ronnie (Popeye) Adams, Jason Rodgers, Roy Benner, and April (Bucket Woman) Richardson.

Also, thanks to the people who helped but didn't want their names mentioned. I can't blame them! But, thank you, thank you.

AUTHOR'S DISCLAIMER

In this era of rampant litigation, we are constantly forced to try to protect people from *themselves*. With that in mind, here are some things you need to know:

1. A five-gallon bucket, like any large container, can be hazardous to small, unsupervised children. If it's left filled with water, a curious toddler can tumble into it headfirst.

A government panel even recommended to the industry, at one time, that they put *restricting devices* in the openings, and *escape apertures* in the bottoms of buckets. Of course, this would mean that you couldn't put a product *in* it, or if you could, you couldn't get it out. Also, that *escape aperture* (known as a *hole* in nongovernment language) would create some rather obvious problems for manufacturers and shippers of *liquids*. They settled on a child-warning label now being placed on buckets.

2. Plastic is *porous and absorbs some of whatever's put in it*. So don't put *food* in a bucket that previously contained poisonous stuff.

3. Five-gallon buckets are made of high-density polyethylene. That means that they can *burn*. Okay?

All I'm saying is this: I don't hurt people with my buckets, and I hope you won't either. If you do, IT'S NOT MY FAULT!

INTRODUCTION
The bucket brigade: How it all began.

It all started innocently enough, when a friend gave me one of those plastic five-gallon buckets. He's in the drywall business, so he was always toting his empties around in the back of his pickup, looking for some sucker to take them off his hands.

The first bucket he gave me was a fine specimen—sturdy, yet sleek. I couldn't imagine throwing it away. After all, it was ideal for washing the car, and often served just that purpose. Then it sat quietly in the corner, awaiting its next use. So, when my buddy offered me another, just like it, I gladly accepted.

Thanks to the genius of some designer's forethought, my new bucket nested neatly inside my first. I quickly pointed that out to my wife when she objected, saying that we didn't need another one. I think she sensed my growing addiction even then.

Having found a ready and willing sucker and a new repository for his endless supply, my friend now inundated me with buckets. He would sometimes leave them at my door, quietly in the middle of the night, like a summer's bumper crop of zucchini. He knew I wouldn't turn them away. By then, I had begun to discover the countless uses to which this marvelous container could be put.

As the ideas, like the buckets, accumulated, I decided that it was time to share this information with the world. Thus, this book was born, as a tribute to the five-gallon bucket, the *ultimate recyclable,* and as an attempt to educate people to its unlimited potential. We *must* do something with them; there are, after all, some *250 million* manufactured every year. I can't handle all of them by myself.

#1
THE BANK-JOB BUCKET
This is a stickup! Oops! Aaaaah!

I won't swear this actually happened, but a buddy of mine who's a cop says it did. This should serve as a warning if you plan to try something similar.

It seems that this felon, after stopping at a couple of bars, decided to rob a small-town bank. As he pulled into the bank's parking lot, he realized that he didn't have anything to serve as a mask. With reasoning muddled by several six-packs, he hit upon the perfect disguise. And everything he needed was right in the back of his truck.

With his rechargeable saw, he quickly cut two eyeholes in a five-gallon bucket. Slipping this over his head, with the handle looped under his chin, he shoved the bank's doors open and took a step forward.

Unfortunately, he forgot his added height. He struck his head on the top of the doorjamb, and the bucket was knocked backward. At that moment, the doors swung back into place, leaving him on the inside with the handle around his neck, and the rest of the bucket on the outside. This is a decidedly awkward position for a would-be bank robber. The two-officer police force, although not used to this type of crime, had little difficulty in making the arrest when the criminal regained consciousness.

3

#2

THE BETTER BABY-BOOSTER BUCKET

If the kid could reach his plate, maybe some of the food would make it to his mouth.

If you live in a small town like I do, your phone book just isn't thick enough to boost a child up to the dinner table.

Here's a plan for a sturdy booster seat that you can make in a few minutes. I won't give you measurements because the size of the child, height of the chair, and design of the table will dictate just how much of a boost is needed.

Use a felt-tip marker to draw the pattern on a five-gallon bucket (as with *most* of the plans in this book, three-and-a-half or even seven-gallon varieties can be substituted) and cut it out with your jigsaw. A piece of foam rubber, an old pillow, or some folded cloth can serve as a cushion. Sand the cut edges smooth or cover with a colorful tape to protect tender skin.

You might put a piece of nonskid rug pad under the bucket to keep it from sliding around, too. Now, EAT THAT SPINACH!

#3
THE DRIBBLING-TIMER BUCKET
Hey, Boss! When do we get our two-and-a-half-gallon break?

Let's suppose you're the foreman on a construction job and it's time for everyone to take a half-hour lunch break. Then you discover that your watch has stopped, and yours is the only watch in the crew. (It could happen.) What do you do now? How can you demonstrate that superior intellect which qualifies you for being the boss?

Just take an 8d nail and punch a hole in the bottom of a five-gallon bucket near the edge. Stick the nail back in the hole from the inside and fill the bucket with water. Now, set the bucket so that it's inclined toward the hole, but so the hole's not obstructed. Next, reach in and pull out the nail. (If it's really cold outside, make the *new* guy do it.)

It will take thirty minutes for the bucket to empty. Of course, since no one has a watch, it might be hard to convince those other guys. Also, if you time the rest of the workday like this, some *bucket watcher* will keep running over to check the water level.

NOTE: Even though this method of timing is quite accurate, it is *not* recommended for use in most offices.

#4
THE BLUSHING BRIDE'S BUCKET
Oh! How nice. A large plastic container.

If you do this, I promise you that your gift will *not* be forgotten and *will* be appreciated. It won't be the most expensive gift at the reception or shower, but it will be the most *original*.

Spray a bucket with gold or silver paint. Squirt some glue on it and sprinkle it with sparklies. Put a big bow on top and pack it full of those things a new couple will need, but no one else will give them. A few suggestions:

- A spatula
- Dishcloths
- A corkscrew
- A meat thermometer
- Rubber gloves
- A manual can opener
- Steak knives

You get the idea. There's a million things newlyweds will find useful after the honeymoon. (There might be a few things in there they'll find useful *during* the honeymoon!)

#5
THE SPUDS-'N'-ONIONS BUCKET
Ahhh. We can breathe.

Ever wonder why the potato bag has that little window, and why onions come in a netlike sack? It's because they keep better if air is allowed to circulate around them. You can *buy* stackable, plastic bins for your pantry, or you can easily make your own with two five-gallon buckets.

1. Cut one bucket off about an inch below the bottom of the shoulder.
2. Place that on top of a piece of wood that will serve as a bottom, and mark the circumference of the bucket on the wood from the inside.
3. Cut out the circular piece of wood, push it into the cut-off bucket, and tack it in place all around. The onion bin is *finished!*
4. Using a jigsaw, cut a scooped opening in a second bucket. This is your potato bin. Note that you can reach in and remove potatoes without removing the onion bin that's stacked on top.

#6
THE MR. ROBOTICO BUCKET
If I only had a brain.

I think I've got the outside perfect. It's the *insides* that are giving me trouble. So far the only thing he'll do is scratch his butt and give me dirty looks.

Even so, my neighbor has offered me an even swap for his youngest son. He says I'll hardly notice the difference except for the increase in my grocery bills.

#7
THE BO JANGLES BUCKET
Bucket stilts will speed up the job.

Remember the last time you painted a room? Remember how hard it was painting that space where the ceiling and the walls join? You've got to use a brush there. Right? And you have to keep moving the ladder around, and going up and down.

You can speed up that process a whole lot by duct taping your feet to the tops of two inverted buckets. It gives you just the reach you need. You can move freely around the room without stopping to reposition a ladder every few feet.

Not only that, but if you can *tap dance* even a *little* bit, you'll be amazed at the effect bucket stilts will have on the performance.

15

#8
THE YOU-CAN-BUDGET-BUT-YOU-CAN'T-BUDGE-IT BUCKET
They can't say YOU don't have any cents!

Almost everyone has a jar, a jug, or *something* that they save pennies in. I don't know why we do it. Perhaps it's a holdover from the time when you could actually *buy* something with a penny. Have you ever noticed that most folks, when they spot a one-cent piece on the ground, won't even bother to bend over and pick it up?

If, on the other hand, you're one of those rare people who *do* pick them up, and compulsively *save* them, then you need something to save them *in*. A five-gallon bucket is ideal for that purpose. It'll hold about *22,700* of them. It's unlikely that a burglar will abscond with them, too. A bucket of pennies will weigh in at around *160 pounds,* and the bottom will fall out if it *is* lifted.

#9
THE MERCEDES BUCKET
Oh Lord, won't you buy me a Mercedes-Benz?!

After you've saved your first bucketful of pennies, the next *219 buckets* are easy. We're only talking five million pennies. Give or take a few buckets. You can *always* talk them down a few *gallons*.

And don't worry about the bottoms of your buckets falling out when you're ready to haul them to the local dealership. With *thirty-five thousand pounds* of copper, the bottom of your *house* is going to fall out, long before you try to move them!

#10
THE BOLD GELATIN-MOLD BUCKET

The dessert that ate Pittsburgh.

Wanna make a hit at the next party? Did you promise to make something *special* for dinner at your mother-in-law's? Do you just like to watch things *jiggle?* Okay, we won't get into that.

Get yourself one of those *food service* buckets and forty packages of gelatin dessert mix. Dissolve the mix in ten quarts of boiling water and then add seven and a half quarts of cold water. Now, chill the monster until firm. Unless you have access to a really *big* refrigerator, you might have to wait for a cold spell to try this.

Finally, once the gelatin is set, run a knife blade around the upper edge and set the bucket in a tub of warm water to loosen it. Invert on a *huge* platter. Stand back and wait for the applause . . . or the *avalanche!*

#11
THE ARCHER'S PRACTICE BUCKET

Oh, it causes me to *quiver* just thinking about it.

Seriously, I do *not* advocate shooting apples or other fruits or vegetables off the tops of people's heads. This a terrible waste of food.

If you're target practicing with a bow, however, you need something to hold your arrows at the ready so that you can easily reach them. A five-gallon bucket is ideal. Placed beside you, and filled with arrows, it allows you to easily grab the next one.

NOTE: That's pointy end *down*.

#12

THE INDISPENSABLE DISPENSER BUCKET

Let's tie one on!

Sociologists studying human behavior (using *millions* of dollars in government grant money) have estimated that the average person spends 3.2 years of his or her lifetime trying to find a strong piece of rope or twine. Actually, I made that up, but I think it's pretty accurate. And, it didn't cost the taxpayers *anything!*

We need a piece of twine for tying up a bundle of twigs or a pile of newspapers (see "THE BUNDLER BUCKET"), or for securing something to the top of the station wagon. We look and we look. We don't *have* any. We looked in all those same places last week. We look again *anyway*.

Those sociologists have examined *that* behavior, too. They were going to comment on it in some prestigious journal, but they couldn't find their notes from the study, no matter *how* many times they looked in their desk drawers.

We save all those lengths of twine that we get at the home-supply store, and *swear* that some day we're actually going to *buy* a supply. In the meantime, we tie short lengths together and hope the playpen doesn't fly off the top of the car and end up in the middle of the interstate.

As for myself, I finally decided to do something about it, and went to my local "farm" store to buy some baling twine (there's nearly *two miles* on one of those spools). While there, I noticed they had a small keg hung from a rafter. A length of string protruded from a hole in the bottom. Back home I copied this design for a string dispenser with a five-gallon bucket. I'll *never* run out of string again!

#13
THE ABOUT-A-YARD BUCKET
It might not be exact,
but it's close enough for gov'ment work.

You're on a construction site, and the excavator is here with the bulldozer. You forgot your tape measure. Say, aren't you the same guy who uses a bucket of water to time lunch breaks? I don't think I want you building a house for *me*.

As luck would have it, you *do* have a five-gallon bucket. Exhibiting that ingenuity which you're now noted for (not to mention your flat-out *weirdness*), you pop the top off the bucket, grab a nail and a stick, and *make* a surprisingly accurate measuring device.

1. Drive a nail through the center of the lid and into the stick near one end.
2. Make a mark on the stick *and* the outer rim of the bucket lid.

Now, just push the stick and the rotating lid along the ground. As the marks pass each other, one revolution (equal to about three feet) has been made. You've covered a distance of one yard.

Obviously, that isn't a precision instrument you've got there, but it *is* accurate enough for a very close approximation.

#14
THE BIRTH CONTROL–DEVICE BUCKET
I don't care WHERE you take 'em!!

"**Y**ou can pound on them, saw them in half, or drill holes in 'em. You can stick your head in one and sing," my wife recently told me. "But if you don't get some of these ##&$@&#!! buckets out of the garage"—like she asked me nicely two weeks ago—"so I can get my car in, you can just sleep on the #@!!*&%@ couch until you *do!*"

Of course, this didn't *really* happen.

#15
THE FISH-OR-CUT-BAIT BUCKET
I can't go fishin' without my lucky bucket.

Next to the bait (and the beer), the one thing you don't ever want to forget when you go fishing is a five-gallon bucket. I don't know how we ever fished without them. Here are a few ways you can put a bucket to use on the next expedition to your favorite fishing hole:

1. Makes a nice dry stool to sit on when fishing from the bank.
2. Holds your bait.
3. Holds your catch.
4. Holds your lunch and drinks. Well, maybe not your bait, your catch, *and* your lunch.
5. If you make some marks on the side, it serves as a ruler for quick measurement.
6. Can be used to bail out the boat.
7. With the lid, it makes an emergency life preserver.

If you come home empty-handed, you can claim that you had a bucket *full* of fish, but one of the really *big* ones flopped around and turned the bucket over.

#16
THE JACK-O'-BUCKET
Ooooh. Scary!

Next Halloween, decorate your front porch with this version of the traditional jack-o'-lantern. It might not frighten off all those little goblins, but they'll figure that if you're too cheap to even buy a *pumpkin* you're no doubt too cheap to give out treats. Eat the candy *yourself!*

#17
THE CHANGE-YOUR-OIL-EVERY-30,000-MILES BUCKET
Or did that owner's manual say 3,000? Whatever.

A nice, reusable container that will hold all the oil you drain from your car can be easily made from a five-gallon bucket.

1. Measure up from the bottom, about seven inches, and mark several places around the outside.
2. Saw the bottom section off. For this project, your cut doesn't have to be all that neat. Don't throw that top half away, though. We'll make use of that later.
3. You can add a few inches of kitty litter to the container to absorb oil if you like.

The *flexibility* makes it a perfect receptacle when you have to change the oil in your lawn tractor, and don't want to totally *disassemble* it to do so.

NOTE: Run your engine a little to heat up the oil, so that when you drop the drain plug into the bucket you can burn your fingers trying to retrieve it. This is a *manly* ritual you ladies just wouldn't understand.

#18
THE CAR-WASH BUCKET
Wash the car. *Please* wash the car.
WASH THAT CAR DAMMIT!

If you ask ten adults to think of a use for a five-gallon bucket, about eight of them will immediately reply, "Washing the car."

Strangely, when asked the same question, most teenagers *cannot* think of this use unless the family car's going to be borrowed for a hot date. (Sexy photos like this sell books.)

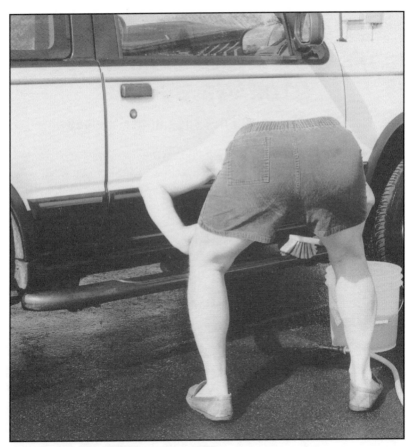

#19
THE STACKABLE-SEASONABLE-STORAGE BUCKET

These things will not slide under the bed.

My wife likes to store winter clothes in the summer, and summer clothes in the winter. This frees up hanger space in the closet. A few years ago I went out and paid lots of money for some of those big flat plastic storage boxes that fit under the bed.

If you've got to slide those flat storage containers out periodically so that you can clean under the bed, the "convenience" of those boxes becomes questionable. To be honest, though, I guess most of us have whole *colonies* of "dust bunnies" thriving under there. I've wondered if we would be more conscientious about cleaning these areas if those balls of fluff had been given a name less *cute*. What if we knew them as dust *rats?* How about dust *warthogs?*

Anyway, the idea of a plastic container with a tight-fitting lid *is* great for storing clothes, but it doesn't have to be flat and cost a lot. Did you know that you can stack about five buckets in the corner of a closet *under* the shelf. You might also line them up along the back wall and put shoes and slippers on them. If you feel creative, you can stack two, place a round or square board on top, drape with fabric, and they'll double as bedside night tables in the spare bedroom.

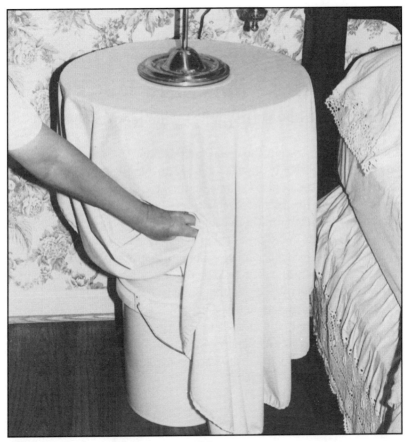

#20
THE V-V-V-I-B-B-B-RATING
WASHING-MACHINE BUCKET

Socks take about fifty miles, blue jeans a hundred.

I can't honestly take all the credit for this one. The great author John Steinbeck wrote about a similar method in his roadtrip book, *Travels with Charlie*. I *can* vouch for its performance, though (as if you might doubt Steinbeck's word, but accept *mine*).

Those of you who travel in campers (excuse me, *motor homes*) will agree that, except for the really *big* ones, they contain all the conveniences of home *except* a clothes washer. Obviously, such an appliance is not practical for most of these vehicles, but a lightweight device that washes your laundry while you drive sounds pretty good, huh?

Just put your soiled clothing in a five-gallon bucket with a little detergent and water, and strap it to the rear of the camper. When you arrive at your next destination, the vibrations of the road will have agitated everything clean. Then rinse and hang up to dry. Now, if we could figure out how to do the *dishes*.

#21
THE ALEXANDER GRAHAM BELL BUCKET
Hello. Hello? Hellooo!!!

Remember how, as a kid, you strung two tin cans together with a string to make a crude telephone? You pulled the string real tight and one of you shouted into one can while the other listened on the other end?

Youngsters who are used to battery-powered toys, and whose idea of communication is "E-mailing" their friends, might find this concept too weird to imagine, but they might learn something about how all that technology got started.

1. Drill a small hole in the centers of two bucket bottoms and run a strong twine through the holes, knotting it on the insides.
2. With each person holding a bucket, walk away from each other until the string is quite taut.
3. Insert your entire head in the bucket and speak loudly.

Your voice vibrates the diaphragm (the bucket bottom), which "amplifies" the vibrations, passing them along the twine. The bucket on the other end oscillates at the same frequencies and reproduces the sound.

#22
THE NOT-A-KNOT BUCKET
Even sailors can't tie 'em like that.

Has anything like this ever happened to you? Maybe you're working on the roof or somewhere else up a ladder and you're using a power tool. You go to pull some more of the extension cord up but it's too short because it's in a big snarled *knot* down on the ground. You know, sailors can't *cuss* like that either.

Make yourself an extension-cord caddy by doing the following:

1. Cut a two-inch *slit* near the bottom of a bucket.
2. Force the *plug* end of an extension cord through the slit from the inside.
3. Pull enough cord through to reach an outlet.
4. Coil the cord into the bucket. As you pull, only the amount you need will be fed, snarl-free, out of the top of the bucket.

When you're finished, you're almost *forced* to replace it neatly in the caddy, ready for the next time you need it.

#23
THE WHO-PLAYS-HORSESHOES-ANYMORE BUCKET

Ain't this the pits?

When I was a kid, on warm summer evenings, the neighborhood *rang* with the sound of horseshoes striking steel stakes. At least once a week, my dad and a few of his friends would join in a friendly competition. The wives would gather to watch, to cheer their husbands on, and to chat. We would watch for a while, but quickly bored by this slow-moving game, we would scurry off to catch fireflies.

THEN WE GOT A TELEVISION! We never saw the neighbors or the horseshoes *again!* It's rumored that in *some* remote parts of the world, people *still* gather for the camaraderie of face-to-face social contact *and*, on occasion, pitch horseshoes.

If the rumors are true, and *you* live in one of these uncivilized places, you're probably searching for a better way of transporting the paraphernalia of this archaic game from home to the "pits." In some cultures, the horseshoes are worn around the neck and the stakes through the earlobes. If you don't like that idea, then a five-gallon bucket makes a suitable carrier.

Oh, and if you see any of my old neighbors, tell 'em "Hi" for me.

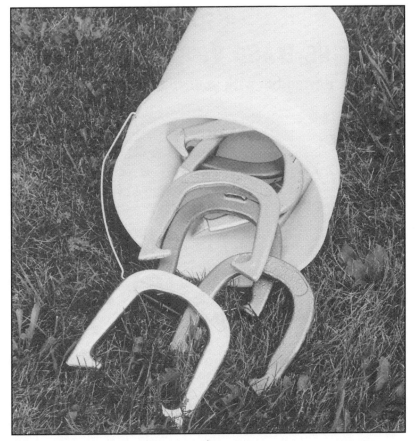

#24
THE BASE VIOL BUCKET
Having fun with your toilet plunger.

Are the children bored? Make them a bass. No, not a *fish!* Don't you people have *any* culture? I mean *a bass (base) viol;* a viola de gamba. All right, I had to consult an encyclopedia to know what to call this thing.

Regardless of *what* you call it, it's going to make music and keep the little ones entertained for *hours.* Well, maybe not hours. Nothing holds their attention that long, except for especially violent TV programs.

1. Drill a small hole in the bottom of a bucket near an edge.
2. Attach a screw eye to the handle of a toilet plunger near the end.
3. Tie a piece of strong twine to the eye and pass it through the hole in the bucket, knotting it on the inside.
4. Place the suction cup against the bucket's bottom and pluck.

By varying the tension on the handle of the plunger, different notes can be achieved. Plunk, *plunk,* PLUNK? Oh, come on. What did you *expect?*

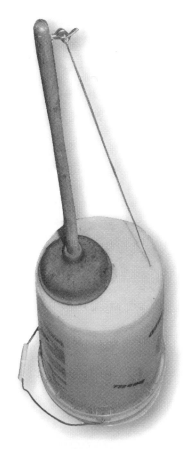

#25
THE BACHELOR BUCKET
When interior decorators have nightmares, this is what they see.

You don't have to have a lot of money to furnish your first home. Five-gallon buckets can be a lovely addition to any fine domicile. And where *else* are you going to get a footstool or end table that saves you trips to the refrigerator by holding an entire Super Bowl game's supply of beer?

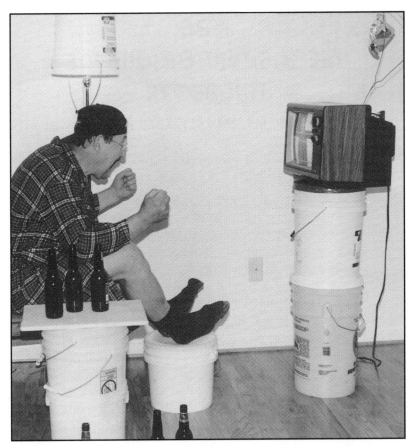

#26
THE BISCUIT/BRIQUETTE BUQUETTE
Feed me, feed me, FEED ME!

Okay, since I'm cheating a little by just telling you what to put *in* a bucket on this one, I'll give you *two* ideas for one low price.

1. *Dog biscuits/pet food*—Don't you wish you could get as excited about *your* dinner as the average dog? My wife's a great cook, but I don't jump up and down and shake my tail and slobber on the floor when she says, "Dinner's ready." Well, only when she makes that tuna casserole I like so much.

   But since pets' food *is* so important to them, you need to keep it nice and fresh and free of pests. Storing it in five-gallon buckets will do that. You can even leave it in the garage or on the back porch instead of the pantry.

2. *Charcoal briquettes*—One of the reasons Cousin Dub can't get the charcoal grill fired up when you go over there for dinner is he leaves the charcoal in the bag and stores it in the shed out back, where it absorbs *lots* of moisture. Of course, since he never has enough charcoal lighter fluid on

hand, and he can *never* find a match now that he quit smoking . . .

If you transfer the briquettes from their bag to a bucket, and keep the lid sealed, they stay drier and are a whole lot less *messy* to handle. Try this: Rub a new bag of charcoal all over your best white shirt or blouse. Now do the same with a plastic bucket. See the difference? You actually *did* it? (Sorry, Tasha, wrong bucket.)

#27
THE TAX-AUDIT BUCKET
Uncle Ira Ess wants YOU!

The Internal Revenue Service (this is a *service*?) requires that you retain receipts for deductions you claim. They also suggest that you keep your tax records for a number of years, so that they can come back and question you after you've forgotten all the good lies you made up.

Any good reference book on accounting recommends that you keep *two* five-gallon buckets for a truly organized system of record maintenance. In one of the buckets, you throw every blessed receipt for *everything,* throughout the year. In the other bucket, keep all your old tax returns, where they'll stay clean and neatly organized until you need them or can legally dispose of them. I'm not licensed to give tax advice, but I think the retention period is about 105 years. To be safe, it's probably best if you have them *buried* with you just in case.

#28
THE BOOTS BUCKET
What size bucket do *you* wear?

You just need to run out and get the newspaper, or get something out of the garden. Maybe, like my friend Max, you drop your false teeth into the pigpen. You can't quickly locate your boots and there's mud or snow or . . . worse, to wade through.

You don't need boots for a quick dash to the curb. Grab two buckets and simply step into one with each foot. Grasp the handles and take a walk. I do this all the time, and now the paperboy pretends he doesn't *know* me.

If you feel creative, you can make some wooden toes to attach to the buckets and start *Big Foot* rumors in your own neighborhood.

#29
THE YOU-DON'T-HAVE-TO-BUY-IT BASKETBALL BUCKET

Making *points* with the youngsters.

Kids don't have to have high-tech or expensive toys to have fun. What they *really* like is for you to play *with* them. You can quickly improvise some games with five-gallon buckets.

Cut a bucket off a few inches below where the handles attach and screw or nail it to a fence post, or maybe the wall *inside* the garage for a rainy-day activity. Make it low enough for the shorter players. A standard basketball fits nicely through the bucket *hoop,* and will endure a surprising amount of play before it has to be replaced.

Here are a few more projects to occupy and entertain children:

1. Sew up a few beanbags and let the kids try to toss them into the top of a bucket. Or you can draw a face on the bucket, cut a hole for the mouth, and let them try to toss the bean bags in the mouth.
2. Let them use an old putter and hit golf balls into a bucket lying on its side.
3. Turn the buckets over and play musical chairs.

4. Practice throwing a softball, football, or baseball, using a bucket as a target.

Encourage *them* to come up with ideas. You'll find that they have almost as much fun helping to *make* these games as they do *playing* them. Their minds, as well as their bodies, will get some excercise. And, it'll be *years* before they figure out how cheap you are.

#30
THE BUCKING-SAWHORSE BUCKET
Yee-hah!!

If the painter is through entertaining the plumber with his dance routine, you can borrow the two buckets he's been using as stilts to make a pretty sturdy sawhorse.

Just invert them (without the lids), lay your board across the tops, and saw away. It helps stabilize everything if you stand on the handle as you saw.

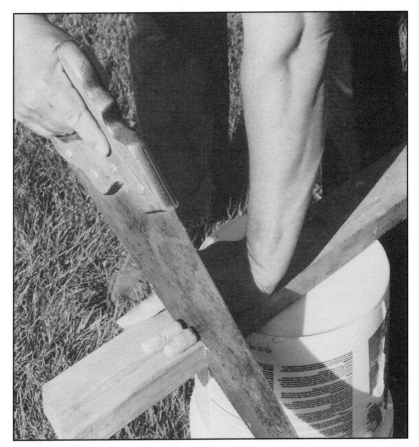

#31
THE BULLROARER BUCKET
If I make a real LOUD noise, will you go away?

A number of aboriginal peoples around the world have, for centuries, employed something known as a "bullroarer" to frighten away evil spirits and their more timid adversaries. It's a slat of wood carved in such a way that when whirled rapidly around it makes a loud, menacing, *roaring* noise. The faster it's spun, the louder the noise.

You know that sound that's produced when you blow across the mouth of a bottle or jug? Wouldn't a much larger container make a much *louder* noise? I reasoned that it would, and that the principle of the bullroarer was the best approach.

Simply tie a strong rope to the handle of a bucket and whirl it around your head like *crazy!* If it doesn't make any scary sounds, lengthen the rope and try again. If it *still* doesn't work, hold the rope in both hands and spin your entire body around.

I tried this, and you might be amazed to learn that it doesn't make *any* noise at all. Surprisingly though, this activity *does* frighten your enemies. It also scares your family, the neighbors, and any passersby who happen to witness it. It's especially effective if you become dizzy and fall on the ground screaming profanities.

#32
THE FINGER-LICKIN'
CHICKEN-KICKIN' BUCKET
Is there someone here by the name of Sal Monella?

You've been *volunteered* again to help with the cooking at the annual office picnic and you've got a *lot* of chicken (fish, softshell crabs, rattlesnake meat, etc.) to flour and fry. Using the same idea as your mama did when she shook chicken parts in a paper bag filled with seasoned coating (I tried that once and just recently discovered a chicken leg that's been behind the refrigerator for twelve years), you can prepare large quantities using a five-gallon bucket.

Using a "food-grade" bucket (not the one you washed the car with), throw in a few pounds of flour, some salt and pepper, and enough chicken to fill the bucket about halfway. Snap the lid on and lay the bucket on its side. Now kick it back and forth between yourself and that other lucky *volunteer*. Everything comes out evenly coated. Just like in your kitchen, you should *never* save the flour for use later on, though. Food poisoning is *no picnic*.

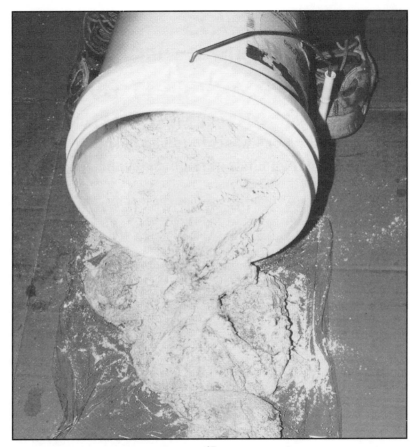

#33

THE HIDE-YOUR-STUFF-WHERE-EVERYONE-CAN-SEE-IT BUCKET

**They might steal the CD player or the radio,
but no one wants to run away with
eighty pounds of joint compound.**

The popularity of sport utility vehicles and minivans has led to a problem. The absence of a trunk means that everything *inside* can be seen from the *outside*. My vehicle has one of these clever things, sort of like a window shade, that rolls out to "conceal" things stored in the back. Of course, no thief would *ever* think that something's *under* that gadget!

Rather than tempt the would-be crooks, I now leave anything I want to hide right out in full view. Well, actually, inside a bucket clearly labeled "drywall joint compound" or "driveway sealer." It won't fool everyone, but come on now—how smart is your average crook?

#34

THE BRING-ON-THE-BRATWURST BUCKET

If you love the aroma of fermenting cabbage . . .

You can have this recipe. But only if you promise to use a "food-service" bucket. Okay? Now get a pencil so I can give you the list of ingredients. Ready? Cabbage, salt . . . Can you remember that?

1. Remove the outer leaves and quarter the heads.
2. Shred the cabbage.
3. Mix about five pounds of the shredded cabbage with three and a half tablespoons of salt.
4. Pack the salted cabbage into the bucket.

Repeat this, five pounds at a time, until you've made more than you could *possibly* ever use or give away. Then, cover the top layer with a clean cloth, put a large plate on top of that, and weigh the whole mess down with a clean quart jar filled with water.

Every day, remove the disgusting scum that forms on the top. Wash and *scald* the cloth before you replace it. It'll ferment like this for about two weeks. After that, it can be packed into jars and processed in a canner. Then you can store it down in the cellar with Aunt Vivian's pickled rutabaga (circa 1964, which *was* an exceptionally good year for rutabagas).

#35
THE CLAMBAKE BUCKET

Get out the stewpot, Mama.
We're havin' *chowda* tonight.

I've only met one ardent clam digger in my limited travels, and he *detested* clams. He said he couldn't imagine why anyone would eat such a disgusting critter, but he just *loves* diggin' the nasty little boogers up.

"Bill," I once asked him, "if you don't like to eat 'em, why do you spend so much time gettin' 'em?"

He told me that, being a simple man, he did it because it's an activity that requires so little equipment: something to dig with, a five-gallon bucket to put them in, and a half pint of relatively inexpensive whiskey.

"Given enough whiskey," he said, "I *can* sometimes be induced to eat one. Of course, given enough whiskey, I could also be induced to eat my *hat!*"

#36
THE CLASSY-CLUNKER DRIP-PAN BUCKET

Out, out, damned spot!

–Shakespeare

Tired of those ugly black oil spots in your garage? GET A NEW CAR! Just kidding. The cheaper solution is to make a drip pan.

1. Measure up from the bottom of a bucket, about six inches, and mark around the outside.
2. Cut the bucket off at these marks.
3. Fill about half full with kitty litter or other absorbent material (like sawdust, for instance).
4. Just slide this under your vehicle at the point of the oil leak.

Say, isn't this just like the oil *change* bucket? For those of you who have been paying attention, and think that you've caught me repeating uses, please note that I said *six* inches for this one, not *seven*. Give me a break. Okay?

#37
THE BIG-EAR BUCKET
Super powers!

Maybe you've seen this done in some old movie, or maybe you've even tried it yourself. By placing an ordinary drinking glass against a wall and then pressing your ear to the bottom of the glass, you can hear what's going on in the next room.

Of course, I've only tried this as an experiment, as listening to a conversation in such a clandestine manner is an invasion of privacy. That's bad! BAD!

But, just for fun, you can employ the same sneaky tactics on a much larger scale, using a five-gallon bucket. You can hear through walls!

When I tried it, I was *amazed!* Not to discover that I could hear what people were saying on the other side of the wall, but that people really *don't* talk about me when I'm not in the room.

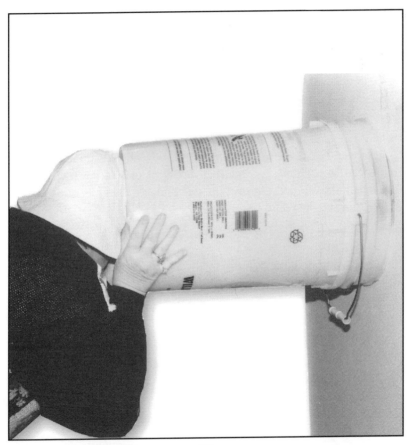

#38
THE YO-YO-BUCKET BUCKET
What goes down, must come UP!

I'm not sure if today's kids know what a yo-yo is. It doesn't use batteries, make interesting noises, or operate in kilobits per second.

For those of us with simpler minds, those who grew up in times less influenced by technology, a toy that just went up and down was pretty exciting stuff. Well, we've grown up now, and our thoughts must turn to bigger things. Like really *huge* yo-yos!

1. Get two bucket lids and a short length of one-inch wooden dowel.
2. Cut a section of dowel about an inch long.
3. With a heavy-duty stapler (or tacks), fasten the two lids to the dowel.
4. Tie a piece of heavy twine around, and wind it up, on the dowel.

Loop the twine around your middle finger and allow the yo-yo to drop of its own weight. With a little practice, you'll become proficient at making this toy go *up* and *down*. What could possibly be more thrilling than *that?*

#39
THE KING-KHUFU BUCKET
No, *cornbread* are square.

Naturally, you recall that pi is the ratio of the circumference to the diameter in any circle, and that pi is equal to 3.14159, rounded to five places. Right? But the following, although difficult for some to accept, are also *true* facts. I'll stake my reputation as an Egyptologist on them.

The pyramids of Egypt were constructed some five thousand years ago with astonishing accuracy. When measurements of these great monuments are made, some of the same numbers that appear in the value of pi mysteriously show up in *these* measurements.

For instance, each side of the Great Pyramid of Cheops (Khufu) measures *exactly* 755 feet. A five appears twice! There's a five in the fourth place after the decimal in the value of pi! Coincidence? Wait! There's *more!*

A five-gallon bucket is circular, which means that pi could be used to calculate its diameter and circumference. Another coincidence?

We are lead to conclude inarguably then, that the ancient Egyptians not only had access to higher math, but to five-gallon buckets as well. It follows logically that these buckets were transported to earth by *aliens* from some distant galaxy.

Therefore, the existence of five-gallon buckets on earth today *proves,* without a shadow of a doubt, the existence of intelligent life beyond our world!

#40
THE BONE-SHATTERING THREE-LEGGED-RACE BUCKET

If there's nothing better to do, you can always hurt yourself.

This concept is not new. When people become bored doing ordinary things, they often try something dangerous. Look at skydiving, bungee-jumping, and hang gliding. Well, *nothing* tops *three-legged bucket racing* for sheer risk!

On a hot summer day a few years ago, after Chuck, Jonesey, and I had been forced to consume an inordinate amount of beer to ward off dehydration, we came up with the idea for this perilous sport. Unlike the old version, which simply has two people bound together by one leg each, three-legged *bucket* racing actually requires *three* legs; one from each of three participants. Each person inserts a leg inside a single five-gallon bucket. They then race against a similarly hobbled team.

NOTE: Broken bones or, at the least, severely barked shins, are a definite hazard of this (soon to be Olympic) sport.

ANOTHER NOTE: Finding three people willing to join in this activity might be fairly easy. But if you're able to come up with *six* to form two competing teams, you're hanging around with a very strange crowd.

Seen here: The rare three-legged-*butcher* race.

#41
THE CLEVER-CRAFTER'S BUCKET
Have you seen my burgundy rose?

For centuries, the term *craft* referred to an enterprise performed by a skilled artisan, a *craftsman*. My dictionary now defines it like this: Craft: Any activity that involves the use of white, runny glue and the painting (in *country* colors) of hearts, flowers, or cute little bunny rabbits on unfinished pine.

My wife enjoys doing crafts, and I'm very tolerant of this pastime. Sometimes though, I wish she would develop an interest in something less *frivolous*, like modifying buckets to make loud, obnoxious noises.

In any case, she makes use of a *lot* of those little bottles of acrylic craft paints, and her need for a constantly growing array of country colors caused her to outgrow the cigar-box container she was using. The bottles were always tipping over or ending up on the floor. Do you have any *idea* what happens when you *step* on one of those things?

When she threatened to *buy* something to corral all those paints, I quickly sawed the bottom off a bucket for her.

The lower two inches of a five-gallon bucket makes an ideal holder for about forty of the common two-ouncers. A tin can, fastened in the middle with a nut and bolt, makes a good brush holder, too.

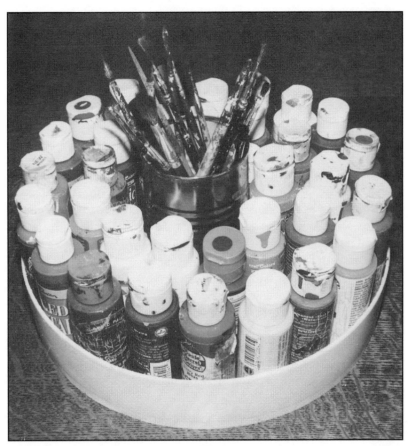

#42
THE SQUAWKING-BLASTER BUCKET

NOT a pretty sound.

Some time ago, I heard a joke about a farmer who administered an enema to his prize bull with a *bugle*. As I recall, the bull is drowned when a drawbridge operator mistakes the bull's flatulence for a steamboat whistle, and raises the bridge as the frightened bull is charging across.

This particular bucket use doesn't have anything to do with steamboats or constipated livestock, but it's as close as I can come to describing the *noise* this thing will make.

You know that irritating screech that's emitted when a drinking straw is drawn up and down through the lid on a paper cup? Do you remember when, after driving about eight hours and everyone was tired and irritable, how the kids in the backseat kept *doing* that?! Remember, you yelled, "HEY! Do you want me to STOP THIS CAR?!" Of course they wanted you to stop the car. They were bored out of their little minds.

Well, now you can get even. You cut two slits in the lid of a bucket, making it resemble that soda-cup lid. Then you get a length of pipe, and when the kids are watching their favorite cartoon on TV, you stick the pipe through the bucket lid and move it up and down like the soda straw.

#43
THE EEE-I-EEE-I-OH BUCKET
. . . and on that farm he had a . . . guess what?

I challenge you to find a farm anywhere that doesn't have a few five-gallon buckets in use. If there's anywhere they come in handy, it's in this setting.

Now, the only dyed-in-the-wool farmers *I* know are the good folks pictured here. They've experienced every agricultural advance since the steam-powered threshing machine, and they will tell you that the most versatile of *all* the inventions that make life on the farm a little easier is the five-gallon bucket.

Actually, *he* would say that it's the air-conditioning, radio, and power steering on that big four-wheel-drive tractor. For the sake of this book, however, I'm taking liberty with his wording. He did say, when pressed for an answer, "They *do* come in kinda' handy." Here are a few common uses:

- Carry in the firewood and kindling
- "Slopping" the hogs and carrying feed and water to the livestock
- A milking stool
- Bringing in a sample of corn to test for moisture content
- A counterweight (filled with rocks) on the shed door
- Nail a lid to the top of a fence post to slow weathering
- Carry the pruning shears and lopping saw to the orchard
- Hauling fencing tools out to the pasture

#44
THE QUICK-DRAW BUCKET
I think I just *wet* myself.

Well, that's one of the hazards of playing with guns. Water guns, that is. You've probably heard of the sport called "paintball," where mature adults run around in simulated combat, shooting at each other with projectiles that splatter when they make contact, marking the opponent as a "casualty."

I'm not sure that this sport's entirely appropriate for young impressionable minds. Far too violent, if you ask me. On the other hand, people of *all* ages and cultures enjoy squirting each other with water guns. It's well known that the president carries one with him to state dinners to lighten the atmosphere.

When you add the element of *skill*, it becomes even more fun. Challenge a friend to a duel. Next, each of you straps on a five-gallon bucket, and armed with those new powerful water weapons, holstered in your buckets, face off for a quick-draw contest that ends in a thorough soaking.

#45

THE PEEINNA BUCKET

All the comforts of home.

We rugged, outdoorsy, hunter-gatherer men are not troubled by the lack of certain conveniences sorely missed by our wives and children when roughing it in some wilderness campground. We don't even need toilet paper. A handful of leaves, a pinecone, or the hide of some dead animal suffices for us. We are *tough!*

But, if we want those of a more delicate nature to accompany us on these returns to nature, we have to provide at least *some* amenities. A toilet of some kind is often one of the requirements. A five-gallon bucket can be slightly modified to serve that purpose.

1. Cut the bottom out of a bucket.
2. Cut around the inside of the lid, leaving just a ring that fits over the lip of the bucket. This creates a fairly comfortable seat.
3. Dig a hole (away from camp) so that the bottomless bucket will fit down in it several inches. After use, the "potty" can be moved and the hole refilled.

NOTE: This seems a good time to bring this up. If you're out scouting up buckets, and you find one at a construction site on the trash pile, and the lid's on it, you *don't* want to open that one.

#46
THE SANTA-CALLS BUCKET
You want a book about BUCKETS?
You'll put your eye out, kid!

There's *nothing* more thrilling to a child than to receive a phone call from Santa. You can get a friend to do it, or do it yourself by disguising your voice with a five-gallon bucket.

Simply place your head, and the telephone receiver, inside a bucket. Hold the mouthpiece away from your mouth and speak in a loud voice. The effect is an echo and an odd reverberation. Tell the child it sounds like that because the call's coming all the way from the North Pole!

Also, if you can't afford one of those cellular phones that everyone seems to have today, you can *pretend* you do.

Call your boss and tell him you're going to be late because you're stuck in traffic in a tunnel.

Call your wife. Tell her you won't be home right away because you fell down an abandoned well.

Impress a client. Say you're calling from your private plane.

Get rid of telemarketers. Tell them you can't talk right now because your house is collapsing into a sinkhole.

Intrigue your friends. Tell them you think your phone is tapped.

Answer the phone, "Darth Vader speaking."

If you're devious enough, you can come up with lots more of these. But don't call *me* for suggestions; I think the FBI is listening in on my conversations.

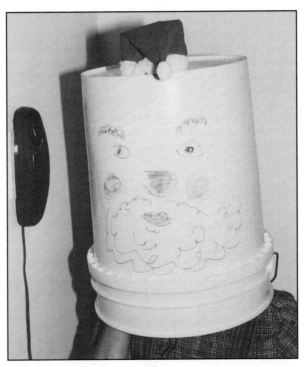

#47
THE WASTE BUCKET
A good place to "file" that sweepstakes entry form.

Did you ever try to find a nice wastepaper basket with some volume? I mean, I make a *lot* of mistakes, and, as a writer, I receive lots of correspondence. Once more, the five-gallon bucket comes to the rescue.

I know what you're thinking. Well, actually I don't. My wife always knows what *I'm* thinking, but that's another story. Anyway, you *might* be thinking that a plastic bucket is just too ugly to serve as a suitable trash receptacle *inside* the house. Of course, without some modification, it is. Here's what you do.

1. Get out that saw and whack another bucket off right below the shoulder.
2. Sand the rough edges.
3. Spray paint it flat black, inside and out.
4. Using a sponge or a ball of crinkled-up newspaper, dab it all over with an earthy, reddish-brown acrylic paint.
5. Coat it with a clear gloss or satin finish.

What you end up with is a classy-looking container that has the same appearance as the dashboard of an expensive European sports car.

#48
THE NEAT FREAK'S HOSE BUCKET
Is it reel?

How do they justify the cost of those hose reels? And how do you put the miserable thing together? I took mine back to the store and got out a bucket, instead. If I could have assembled it I probably *would* have kept it. It had whitewall tires and a CD player.

The bucket is a simpler (no assembly required) and *cheaper* alternative. Just coil the hose into the bucket between uses. If you use them for car washing, they're there together when you need them. If you have to store the hose during the winter, you can hang the whole thing from a hook in the ceiling. You can't do *that* with one of those awkward reels!

#49
THE BLACK BART-OF-BEANS BUCKET
Avoirdupois?

In many parts of the country, you can buy fresh produce at pick-your-own orchards or farms. You save money and you're assured of getting better quality since you do the gathering.

Sometimes these places will furnish you with paper or plastic bags for your purchase. The paper one will get soggy and the bottom will dissolve when you pick it up. The plastic bag collapses in the trunk of your car and allows everything to roll around back there. A plastic bucket is more practical, both for gathering and transporting your harvest.

But beware of being *overcharged* if you use a bucket. At one farm that we used to frequent, string beans were sold by the *peck*. The farmer even had a sign explaining this unit of measurement for us "agriculturally challenged" folks. It read: 4 quarts = 1/2 peck; 8 quarts = 1 peck.

He even furnished five-gallon buckets to his customers to use when picking. If they came back with a full bucket, he'd push back his old straw hat and rub his stubbly jaw, while he calculated out loud.

"Let's see," he would say. "There's four quarts in a gallon; twenty in five gallons. There's eight quarts in a peck, so that means you folks got two and a half pecks in that bucket."

And that's what we paid for. It took me some time to realize we were being short-beaned. You see, 20 *liquid* quarts equals 1,155 cubic inches, while 20 *dry* quarts equates to 1,344 cubic inches. That's a difference of 189 cubic inches, or nearly 3 quarts of farm-fresh, u-pick-'em-yourself-city-boy beans we paid for but left on the vine!

#50
THE CHIHUAHUA-BED BUCKET
Izzu mommiewammie's iddybiddy poochiewoochums?

A very small dog needs a very small bed. The bottom portion of a bucket will make just such a bed.

1. Saw a bucket off about eight inches up from the bottom.
2. Use a marker to draw what you feel is an appropriate opening in one side. This design is similar to that of a wing chair, and serves the same purpose: to block floor-level drafts and keep your pet cozy.
3. Add some soft bedding, like doggie's favorite pillow or a folded blanket.

Let's be honest though, folks, these little lap-warmers rarely have to sleep on the floor, do they?

NOTE: Yes, I'm *aware* that this is not a dog. I was hoping you wouldn't notice. But, if you hold the book out at arm's length and *squint* . . .

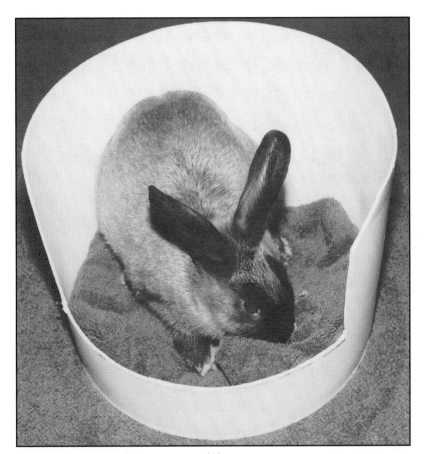

#51
THE MARCH-TO-A-DIFFERENT-BEAT BUCKET

Can you play louder? I think I can still hear with THIS ear.

An acquaintance of mine recently said, "The *second* dumbest thing I ever did was to let my son take up playing the drums."

"What was the *dumbest* thing?" I asked.

"Buying the drums before he decided if he *really* wanted to be a drummer," he replied.

If you have an aspiring percussionist in the family, maybe you should improvise a little at first. Sure, you can go ahead and spring for a *professional* pair of drumsticks. They're not all that expensive, but hold back on the drums for a while.

By substituting five-gallon buckets, and arranging them to duplicate the placement of a *real* set, the young player can gain valuable experience. The sound can be varied by playing with or without a lid, or by playing upright or inverted.

"Since this will *never* really sound like the real thing," you might ask, "couldn't this discourage an aspiring young musician from pursuing this option?"

"Your point *is*?" I would reply. (The cymbals really *suck*!)

#52
THE BUNDLER BUCKET
That's old news.

And once you've read it, you should do your part to see that your old newspapers are recycled. The problem is, in many places they have to be tied up in neat bundles before they'll be accepted by the recyclers. It helps to have something to *hold* the papers as you tie them up. A modified bucket will work nicely.

1. Saw two slots halfway through a bucket, about four inches from each end.
2. Turn the bucket on its side and lay two lengths of strong cord in the slots.
3. As you collect newspapers or other periodicals, just place them in the bucket on *top* of the string.
4. When the bucket is full, pick up the ends of the twine, tie a couple of knots, and remove the secured bundle.

Now, if I could just convince my wife to get rid of some of these old catalogs and magazines. Wait a minute! That's the *swimsuit* issue!

#53
THE IF-PIGS-COULD-FLY BUCKET

How can they *eat* so much?

People, when they first start feeding the birds, are amazed at how much seed is consumed. They soon discover that buying those little bags of birdseed at the grocery store is impractical. Many graduate to buying it in large sacks or five-gallon buckets (you *know* how I buy it).

If you *do* choose to purchase it by the bucketful, you can then convert the empty bucket to a bird *feeder,* following these easy directions.

1. Beginning about four inches from the bottom, cut an arched opening in the side.
2. Replace the lid, fill the bottom with seed, and hang in a tree.
3. If you like, paint the bucket green or brown to make it blend with the foliage.

The birds will enter the bucket, and eat under shelter. This makes a good feeder to place on the ground for birds who don't normally frequent hanging feeders, too.

#54
THE TERRACED-TOMATOES BUCKET

How to plant on a slant.

My neighbor Jack is from Holland, so he knows a little about keeping the dirt where the dirt's supposed to be and the water where the water's supposed to be. He's also one of those meticulous gardeners who make people like me want to go home and start pulling weeds. It's about all I can do to resist this urge sometimes—-but I'm usually successful.

Jack likes to plant a few tomatoes alongside his house, just a few steps from his kitchen. But the ground slopes pretty drastically there. If he planted in that location in a normal manner, watering his plants could be a futile effort.

He solved the problem of planting on sloping ground by cutting the bottoms out of five-gallon buckets and burying them up to their shoulders. Then he filled the buckets with some good topsoil and planted a tomato per bucket. Now, when he waters and fertilizes, each plant gets and retains its share of nourishment.

I'd like to be able to tell you *I* suggested this method to *him*, but there's always the possibility that he might read this book.

#55

THE ALPENHORN BUCKET

If you don't have any cows, it'll fetch the kids.

Herdsmen in the Alps blow a horn that's sometimes as much as twenty feet long, to call in their cattle. The sound these instruments make can be heard for *miles*. Perhaps you don't have any cows, but are once more possessed of a desire to make very *loud* noises.

While those Alpine cowboys use horns lovingly crafted of native woods, we can duplicate their horns with modern materials and next-to-no skill. (This is the type of skill I have in ample supply.)

Using PVC pipe, a few collars, elbows, and a bucket, you can assemble your own version. I don't recommend gluing it together. You *might* want to disassemble and *hide* this thing quickly.

#56
THE FOUNDATION-OF-CIVILIZATION BUCKET

All it *apiers* to be.

As you've seen already, five-gallon buckets are a builder's best friend. Here's one more *legitimate* way in which they can be put to use.

First, some facts. A five-gallon bucket just happens to have a volume of 1,155 cubic inches, while an eighty-pound sack of concrete mix will make two-thirds of a cubic foot of concrete. That's 1,158 cubic inches! Pretty darn close, don't you think? Another coincidence, or further proof that aliens from outer space have interfered with humankind's progress?

But, since there *is* such a good match, a bucket makes an excellent form for pouring concrete when you want a short sturdy column. Such as:

• With the bottom cut out, buried below the surface of the ground, and filled with concrete, the bucket makes a good *pier* for the posts of a deck.

• Or, filled with cement that is allowed to partially set, and then inverted, the buckets create columns for projects like: (1) two with a board on top for a bench; (2) the base of a birdbath; (3) a stand for a large flowerpot; or (4) topped with a piece of tempered glass to make a contemporary table.

#57
THE ALL-YOUR-EGGS-IN-ONE-BASKET BUCKET

Built for a poultry sum.

There was a time when almost *everyone* kept a few chickens, farmers as well as town dwellers. Many farms still do. And in some suburbs, it's still possible. All you need is shelter, food, water, and chickens.

Once you've built the shelter, you'll need to construct nesting boxes for your hens. They aren't all that picky about accommodations, but they *do* like a little privacy when laying eggs.

You can construct them in the traditional manner using wood, or for a lot less expense, five-gallon buckets.

1. Attach buckets, side by side, to the wall of the shelter.
2. Provide some support (like a two-by-four) underneath the buckets, and a roost out front (serves as a landing strip).
3. Fill with straw or other nesting material, and replace a cut-down lid to help retain it.

Aside from the ease and low cost of construction, the bucket-nests have the added advantage of harboring fewer pests than wood, and being easier to clean.

#58
THE FIVE-GALLON-BUCKET
FIVE-GALLON BUCKET

Rollin', rollin', rollin' alooong.

For professional painters, purchasing paint in five-gallon buckets is the only way to go. Not only is it cheaper that way, but for jobs where a paint roller is the tool of choice, the buckets serve both as the holders of *and* the dispensers of the paint.

In any paint store, you can buy a metal grid designed specifically for use in a five-gallon bucket. It's a rectangular mesh with two hooks for hanging over the top of a bucket.

You just dip the roller in the paint (the bucket shouldn't be more than half full to start), and then roll off the excess paint against the grid. There's *much* less spattering than with a tray, and the job is speeded up because you don't have to stop for a refill as often.

Although this won't make you a professional painter, it'll make you *look* like one.

#59
THE BOWL-THEM-OVER-
WITH-WIT BUCKET

You'll be in another league.

Are you in a bowling league? Does your team resemble every other team with matching shirts or jackets? How about matching bowling bags? No? Then it's about time you get it together and come up with something original.

A five-gallon bucket (or the three-and-a-half gallon variety) makes a fine container to carry both your bowling ball and your shoes. Decorate the outside with your team's name, maybe. This tactic will give you a psychological edge, as competing bowlers will suffer from bouts of hysterical laughter every time they see your bowling "bag," causing them to lose control and roll gutter balls.

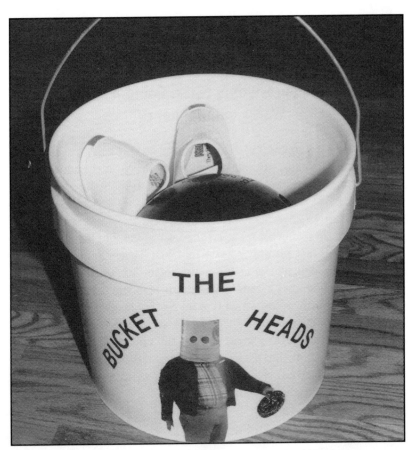

#60
THE BIDDER'S BUCKET
Going once. Going twice. Going *home*?
Wait a minute, honey!

I love attending auctions. I can happily spend an entire day just standing around or rummaging through the junk. My wife, on the other hand, prefers to sit and wait for the auctioneer to get to the items she's interested in. If there's no place to sit, she doesn't like to stay very long. That's why I carry a five-gallon bucket to auctions now.

Not only does a bucket make a comfortable seat, but it conveniently holds snacks, drinks, reading material for when the less interesting items are being auctioned, and wrapping materials for our small purchases. A collapsible umbrella, a hat, and a sweater are sometimes included.

After the lunch is consumed, the bucket is filled with glassware or other things bought during the day. My wife is happy, having her portable *home-in-a-bucket,* and I'm happy because she's not begging me to leave.

There are lots of other places at which one of these buckets will come in handy. I wanted to take one with me when we went to the shopping mall last week, but my wife wouldn't let me.

#61
THE DOWN-'N'-DIRTY BUCKET
Humus be kidding!

I don't have a green thumb. I can never figure out what a plant needs. Does it need fertilizer? Does it need water? If it needs water, why can't it just drink out of the toilet like my dog?

My wife's quite the indoor gardener, though. She's always buying new plants or repotting old ones. We were constantly buying potting soil. That stuff's expensive, and personally, I don't think they put any *dirt* in there. I'm old-fashioned. I think plants *need* dirt.

So, we asked the lady at the nursery if she knew a formula for making our own potting soil. "Sure," she said. "You buy it here, and when you get it home you *make* it come out of the bag."

Eventually we *did* find an ideal formula. Here it is:

1. Sterilize about two gallons of garden soil, by putting it in a metal container and baking at 200 degrees for half an hour.
2. Put the sterilized soil in a five-gallon bucket and add a gallon of *leaf mold*. That's a fancy name for *humus,* which is a fancy name for *composted organic matter,* which is a fancy name for *rotten leaves.*
3. Add a gallon of common builder's sand, replace the lid, and roll until well mixed.

#62
THE BUCKET-GAME BUCKET
Duh, I dunno. I guess you could put sumptin' in 'em.

If you ever get *really* bored, you and a few friends can always play the *bucket game.* The rules are real simple, and you can improvise and make up some of your own. Here's the basic idea:

1. Divide into teams with equal numbers of players. A hint so you don't waste too much time on this step; if there's an *odd* number of people, you *will* have difficulty doing this. Rather than getting involved with these complicated mathematics, just compete as individuals.

2. See how many uses for a five-gallon bucket each team or player can come up with in two or three minutes. The uses can be logical or ludicrous, the only restriction being that you can't simply name things that can be put *into* a bucket.

NOTE: Excessive playing of this game can lead to brain damage or book publication. (Sometimes, as shown here, large groups gather for tournaments.)

#63
THE TRAVELING-TREE BUCKET
It takes a NUT . . .

. . . to grow a nut tree and acorns for oaks. In one area of my property, I'm growing trees, which I started from seeds, in five-gallon buckets. At present I have oak, tulip poplar, cherry, and black walnut. Each bucket is labeled as to the type of sapling it contains, but the grandchildren know them as *first, second, third,* and *home* base. In the fall they're called *goal posts.*

Buckets are ideal for such plantings, since you can move the seedlings around according to weather conditions. Too much snow? Move them to a sheltered area. Drought? Move them closer to a water supply. Remember to punch some holes in the bottoms for drainage. (I think I left this one in the bucket too long.)

#64
THE IT-AIN'T-FORT-KNOX BUCKET
They can't *steal* it if they can't *find* it.

If you're like me, you've got tons of valuable stuff around. Or maybe you have only a few pieces, which for sentimental reasons you would rather some stranger didn't hock at the local pawnshop.

You can make a "safe" from a five-gallon bucket. It's not impregnable; it's just not a likely place for a thief to *look*.

1. Measure the inside diameter of a bucket, down about four inches from the top.
2. Cut a circle of plywood that diameter.
3. Cut a small slot in the board so that the blade of an old putty knife will fit through.
4. Lightly grease the inside of the bucket, and insert the wooden "plug" you cut out.
5. Spread about an inch of drywall joint compound over the wood and around the blade of the putty knife.

After the joint compound has hardened, you can carefully work the plug loose. After that, using the handle of the knife, you can remove and replace what appears to be the surface of a full bucket. Hide your goodies under there. You can rest assured that any self-respecting burglar is going to carefully avoid anything that's normally associated with *work!*

129

#65
THE NO-BRAINER BUCKET
Jack Frost, where be thy sting?

–Sasquatch

This use really didn't tax my mental abilities. I probably spent less than two days, drove no more than two hundred miles, interviewed only six horticulturists, and spent *under* three hundred dollars researching it. (The preceding is for the benefit of any IRS people reading this book.) Here it is just in case you *haven't* thought of it, though.

In areas where late frosts threaten newly planted seedlings, you need some method of protecting them from frostbite. Rolls of plastic, newspapers, and other tricks are employed by gardeners in their efforts to save young plants from the killing effects of dipping temperatures.

Nothing could be better for this task than the five-gallon bucket. Since they nest neatly, one inside the other, a great many of them can be left near the garden for immediate use. Remember, though, that any buckets left outside should have their bottoms pierced so that they don't fill with water and become a hazard to toddlers.

131

#66
THE BRAVISSIMO BUCKET
Why didn't you tell me how GOOD I am?

Do you ever do it in the shower? You know, *sing?* It's funny how good your voice sounds under those conditions. Well, let me tell you, the acoustics inside a five-gallon bucket are even better. They rival those of Carnegie Hall.

NOTE: This is probably one of those things best tried when you're *alone*. Also, if you *do* turn professional, you might find it difficult to hear the band. Thank ya. Thank ya very much.

#67
THE THERE'S-NUTTIN'-
LIKE-KNITTIN' BUCKET
A bucket cozy? Grandma, you *shouldn't* have!

Do you know any knitters? I know a few *nitpickers,* but no one who can turn yarn into clothing. Thousands of you *do* knit, however, or you have family members who do. And everyone who enjoys this hobby needs something to hold and organize their skeins of yarn and knitting needles.

This project is a good one to help the kids with, if they want to make a gift for Mom or someone else special.

1. Cut a bucket off so that it's about ten inches tall.
2. Coat the outside with adhesive that comes in an aerosol spray.
3. Cover the bucket with an attractive fabric, folding the top and bottom edges and the seam *under* for a finished appearance. Fabric glue will seal these folded edges.

Okay, so the kids get a little glue all over everything, and they don't smooth the fabric out *perfectly.* Now *you're* nitpicking.

135

#68
THE WE-KNOW-WHAT-HAPPENED-TO-JIMMY-HOFFA BUCKET

You grab his . . . no, wait . . . I'll pick this up . . . no . . . FORGET IT!

This is a true story. Not long ago, a body was found in the train yard in Baltimore. The victim had been shot and had one foot encased in a bucket of cement. We can envision several scenarios:

1. The perpetrators stuck their victim's leg in the cement with intentions of forcing him down to the nearby harbor, where he would be thrown in to drown. Of course, they would have discovered at that time that it's impossible to make someone with eighty pounds of cement on their foot go *anywhere*. That's when they would have given up and shot him.

2. Or, they might have shot him *first* and then put his leg in the bucket, planning on disposing of the body in the harbor. That's when they would have found that they had the world's most *awkward* package to transport.

If these guys had ever done any three-legged-bucket racing they would have *known* how difficult this endeavor was going to be.

#69
THE YOU-HAD-BETTER-BE-ON-THE-LEVEL BUCKET
Is this how they built that famous tower in Italy?

You need to level an area for the children's wading pool or a small patio, and just "eyeballing" it doesn't seem to be working. You might try the five-gallon-bucket version of the ancient *water level,* known to the Greeks, Romans, and extraterrestrials who helped the pharaohs erect their pyramids.

1. Measure up several inches on the inside of a bucket and make a continuous mark all around the inside with an *indelible* marker.
2. Fill with water to the line. It helps if the water is a little muddy. Ted Bob, an old buddy of mine, uses beer. He says he can see that better. Of course, Ted Bob rarely finishes these types of projects.

Note that when the bucket is placed on a sloping surface, you can easily detect in which direction the surface tilts.

"But this only shows how level the ground is directly below the bucket," you might say, a little sarcastically.

Not if you place the bucket on a straight board laid on the surface, smart mouth!

#70
THE TERRIBLY-TALL-TOP-HAT BUCKET
The hat that tips YOU.

Cowboys, in the old Westerns, wore what everyone came to know as *ten-gallon* hats. Naturally, they weren't *really* capable of holding ten gallons of anything, but *you* can make a hat that really *is* a five-gallon equivalent. This will be a "big" hit at the next costume party (or formal event).

1. Remove the handle from a bucket.
2. Cut a large (about three feet in diameter), circular piece of cardboard or foamboard (available in craft and art stores).
3. Cut out an opening in the center of the cardboard that will tightly fit your head.
4. Attach the cardboard to the rim of the bucket with construction glue.
5. Spray paint the whole thing black.

Yes, Virginia, there really *is* a Mad Hatter!

#71
THE ROCK-'N'-ROLLIN'-CEMENT-MIXIN' BUCKET

Just a little mortar maker.

If you've ever needed to mix just a little mortar or cement for a "patch" job, the first problem you ran into was finding something to mix it in. Maybe you used a wheelbarrow, or even *bought* a tray designed for the purpose. Why not make yourself a cement mixer, instead?

The first thing you'll need is a *large truck chassis* . . . only kidding. All you need for this project is a bucket, its lid, a strip of wood one inch by two inches (and as long as the bucket is deep), and several wood screws.

1. Drill several holes in the bucket's side, and screw the wood strip to the inside. That's it!

Now, just add sand or gravel mix (about half a sack at the most) and some water. Snap the lid on and rock or roll the bucket for a few minutes until the concrete is thoroughly mixed.

#72
THE MASTER-MECHANIC'S-
TOOL-BOX BUCKET
Metric, shmetric, where's my adjustable wrench?

All your life, you wanted a *real* mechanic's toolbox, one of those BIG suckers, with drawers for *everything*—one that sits on a matching cabinet with wheels, so you can roll that rascal right up to the car and have everything you need at your fingertips. So you scrimped and saved, and *finally* bought one, along with all the tools you'll ever need.

Then, the stupid riding mower breaks down out in the middle of the lawn. Are you going to carry that seven-hundred-pound tool chest out to the mower? Maybe you only need one or two wrenches. But is that bolt $13/16$ths or $7/8$ths? You might as well take a good selection out there with you, or you'll just do a lot of running back and forth.

For those situations, you need a smaller toolbox, and a bucket substitutes nicely. It'll hold all the tools you need for an emergency repair. Of course, it doesn't have all those nice little drawers.

#73
THE RAINY-DAY BUCKET
Mary Poppins had one.

Up until the early part of the twentieth century, almost every home had some sort of umbrella stand near the front door. What happened? Did we stop caring that wet umbrellas were being brought into our homes to drip on the floors?

I say we revive the tradition, and put a five-gallon bucket by everyone's front door. Well, okay, the back door then. But it doesn't have to be *unattractive*.

1. Saw a bucket off right below the shoulder, and smooth the edges.
2. Spray it with a brass-colored paint, inside and out.
3. Dip a brush in black paint and then tap it against your hand or a stick held several inches from the bucket. This will speckle the surface and give it an *antiqued* look.

Now that you've made this lovely addition to your home, I've got to tell you something. You don't *have* any of those old-fashioned *long* umbrellas. All the umbrellas today seem to be those little collapsible things. Go out and buy some *real* umbrellas. Get rid of those little sissy things. You've got an umbrella stand!

#74
THE NOT-THE-BUCKET-BOOTS-BUT-THE-BOOTS-BUCKET BUCKET
Not on my clean floor!

Now that you've got something to put the drippy umbrellas in, you think your floors are safe. Right? How about those wet, snowy, muddy boots? You can purchase a rubber tray made specifically for that purpose, but you can make a couple for *nothing*.

All you need is the lower two inches or so of a bucket. This will hold several pairs of children's boots or one pair of average-size adult boots. If you've got big feet like me, you can saw the bucket at an angle, so that the runoff will collect in the bucket bottom, not on the floor.

If you need several, don't worry, they stack nicely when not in use.

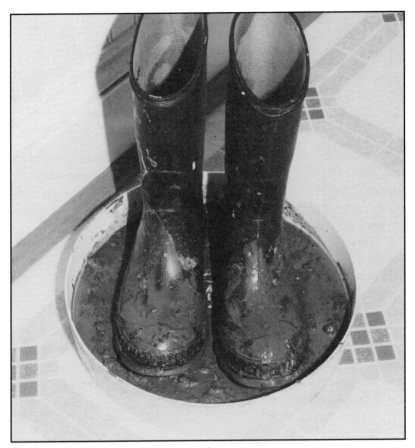

#75
THE YOU-CAN'T-TOP-IT MOP-IT BUCKET
Careful. That floor's w-e-ttt!

We have a dishwasher, a clothes washer, and a self-cleaning oven, but we *still* have to mop the floor. Since we do, a five-gallon bucket certainly surpasses one of those small pails sold for that purpose. Why, you can barely get a mop *in* one of those things, and there's no room for wringing the mop out.

I convinced my friend Ray of this, but he's been unable to convince his wife, Elizabeth. He's tried and tried to show her how much more efficient a bucket is. I witnessed one of his attempts recently.

"Oh, honey, that's too awkward," she said. "Those things are too heavy. They're too big."

"No, look," he insisted. "See how it slides along. See how *neat* it is?"

We chuckled to ourselves later. Even though he had now demonstrated the efficacy of this method to his wife by mopping their kitchen floor the last *twelve* times, she just can't seem to grasp the idea. We men are *so* much smarter.

#76
THE DON'T-MAKE-LIGHT-OF-IT BUCKET

Humbug!

Every year it's the same. You get out those strings of holiday lights and find that, even though you were careful when you put them away last year, they're a tangled mess now. How does this happen? If we sneak up on them in the middle of summer, will we find them writhing like snakes, tying themselves in knots? Perhaps this is a mystery we can never *unravel*.

You can prevent this annual battle of the bulbs if you use a five-gallon bucket when removing and storing these decorations. As you take them down, coil them into the bottom of the bucket. Tag the end of each strand as it goes in. You might hang the bucket from a rafter during the time they're not needed.

Next year, when you're ready to rehang them, you retrieve the tagged end and decorate right out of the bucket. Of course, you can avoid *all* this trouble by just leaving them *up* all year. What? You don't have to turn them *on!* (Uhh, where's that tag?)

153

#77
THE NANTUCKET BUCKET
A fashion statement.
But what is it *saying?*

My wife saw an ad in the back of one of those classy magazines for a little woven basket that's sold for use as a *purse*. It's made in New England and, like *everything* advertised in classy magazines, and made in that part of the country, that sucker's *expensive!* She really wanted one though, and being the type of guy I am, I hate to disappoint her. So, for our anniversary I made her a substitute.

Okay, I agree it's not exactly like the one she wanted, but this purse will hold a lot more. Boy, this turned out a whole lot like that *Birth-Control Bucket.*

#78
THE BIG-BAD-BRIEFCASE BUCKET

Mine's BIGGER than yours.

Wee men, I mean *we* men, are concerned about things like that. And since we are, I decided that my briefcase would be larger than anyone else's.

Throw away those silly backpacks and too-small attachés and get yourself a *man's* briefcase that'll hold all your important papers, several sandwiches, a paperback book (I can suggest one), and your golf shoes. All the other guys at the office are going to suffer *briefcase* envy when you walk in.

#79
THE BRAVE-THE-BLIZZARD BUCKET

Let it snow, let it snow, let it snow.

Every winter, we hear about people being stranded in their vehicles by unexpected snowstorms. Fortunately, most are rescued after enduring hours, or even days, in freezing temperatures with little food, water, or adequate clothing.

A five-gallon bucket in the trunk of your car could mean the difference between survival and tragedy. If you're going to venture out in unpredictable weather during the winter, here's how to make a simple survival kit:

1. Fill a bucket about one-third full of sand. The weight will improve traction in rear-wheel-drive vehicles and can be spread under the tires to get you unstuck.

2. In some of the remaining space, put a tin can, several candles, and some matches. A candle burned *in* the can will warm your hands; burned under the can, it will melt snow for drinking. The can also doubles as a dipper for the sand.

3. Next, add some food, like granola and candy bars.

4. A flashlight, batteries, and signal flares could come in handy.
5. Then, cram in anything else in the way of clothing or blankets that will fit. The bucket itself can be useful in digging your car out of a snowbank.

My advice though, if faced with traveling in this kind of weather, is to leave the bucket at *home* in the trunk of your car, where you *and* your car belong.

#80
THE MR. CLEANGREENS BUCKET
Stand back! I gotta wash this lettuce.

Before we start, let me advise you apartment dwellers to just skip this one. Although this trick *will* work effectively with your salad greens, dinner guests could be seriously injured. While it would demonstrate your cleverness, there are better ways to impress the boss or the in-laws.

You rural gardener types, on the other hand, can save lots of time cleaning leafy vegetables like spinach, kale, and mustard greens with this method.

You need to drill *lots* of holes in the bottom and all around the sides of a bucket. A farmer I know blasts them with a shotgun. He doesn't grow stuff like that, but ever since I let him read a draft of this book, he just *hates* buckets!

After picking, place the greens in the perforated bucket and hose them down several times. After each rinsing, sling the bucket around rapidly by the handle or by means of a rope tied to the handle. Excess water will be thrown off.

Spectators are encouraged to cheer . . . and to *duck!*

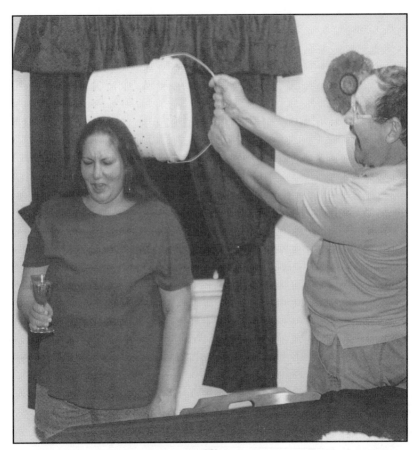

#81
THE BEEN-THERE-BEEN-THAT BUCKET

I'm so old, I remember when we could throw stuff *away*.

Alas, those days are gone. In almost every community today, separating our trash into recyclables or nonrecyclables is either mandatory or, at least, optional. Just last week, two of my neighbors, Peggy and Jim, were dragged off kicking and screaming by the EPA for hiding an empty aluminum can at the bottom of their regular garbage.

What better use to make of the *ultimate recyclable* than to press it into service as a receptacle for everything else you have to segregate into categories for potential remanufacturing. One for glass, one for plastic, and so on. Punch a few holes in the bottoms, so that the beer—uh, soda pop—that's left in the containers, as well as rainwater, can drain out.

I *love* recycling. It means that all my old margarine tubs and plastic soft-drink bottles can be turned into more FIVE-GALLON BUCKETS!

GLASS
ONLY !

163

#82
THE I-LOVE-A-PARADE BUCKET
Please stand for the National Anthem.
Oh, you *are* standing.

My dear wife is under five feet tall. That means that she has missed seeing about a third of everything that's ever happened around her. She recently became a bucket convert after attending a local Independence Day parade.

Our town doesn't enjoy a very fast pace, compared with the rest of the world. It does, however, take every opportunity to show off its patriotism *and* the new fire truck. One of the biggest events is the Fourth of July parade. The problem is, since the main street is only five blocks long, you have to be there *really* early for a good spot right on the curb. If my wife ends up behind anybody, she can't see a thing.

That's why I convinced her to take along a *parade* bucket this year. You'll probably recognize the similarity between this and the *auction* bucket. You can still pack your lunch and cold drinks in it, and you can still sit on it while you wait, but when the time comes, you turn it *over* and stand on it.

For the first time in her life, my wife will hear, "Please sit down. You're blocking my view." (Hon, is this the *third* of July?)

#83

THE PICKY PLUMBER'S PARTS BUCKET

Just keep holding that pipe while I run to the hardware store.

Isn't it frustrating to be in the middle of a job and discover that you don't have the right part to finish it with? Don't you envy the people who have all their little doodads organized?

I'll bet you've seen one of those buckets that plumbers use. They have a tray on top for small fittings, and room underneath for the larger ones. I was admiring one of these, and asked the plumber if he could tell me how he made *his.* He said he would be happy to, but that I would have to make an appointment with his secretary, and that it would cost me thirty dollars an hour to talk to him about it. I designed one *myself!*

1. Saw a bucket off two inches below the shoulder and remove the handle.
2. Using that as a pattern, draw a circle on a piece of wood, and cut out the circular piece.
3. Tack the wood to the cut-off bucket, forming a new bottom.
4. Cut another piece of wood as wide as the cut-down bucket is deep, and as long as the bucket's diameter.

5. Cut another as long, but about three inches wider.
6. Cut notches in the center of each board so they'll fit together.
7. Shape the wider board to make a handle for lifting it; attach the boards to the bottom with glue or nails, and set the *divided* tray inside another bucket. Now you too can earn thirty bucks an hour, and use all the time you want to take, uh, fix, a leak.

#84
THE JARDINIERE-IN-A-JIFFY BUCKET

Ain't that just a big ol' flowerpot?

That's true, today we do refer to them as pots or, even more mundanely, as plant *containers*. But something *this* elegant deserves a more romantic name.

1. Start by cutting a bucket at the height suitable for the plant you're going to put in it.
2. With sandpaper, smooth the sawn edges, and lightly scuff the surface of the bucket.
3. Paint the outside with a light-colored *flat* paint.
4. Using a sponge, and whatever contrasting color suits you, dab all over the previously painted surface. Do the same thing with at least one other color.
5. Dip the end of a feather, or a very thin brush, in white paint and draw random, squiggly lines here and there on the sponge-painted bucket. This simulates the veins in *marble*.

Get some of that potting soil you made earlier and give that faithful old frangipani a new home.

#85
THE WAKE-UP-SCREAMING BUCKET
I'm up. I'm UP!

In another part of this book I told you how to make a *timer* out of a bucket. This time, we'll use a bucket in conjunction with a *real* clock to arouse those heavy sleepers in the family.

Now me, I wake up if the cat passes gas in the next room. Some of you might not sleep that lightly, and you might even snooze right through the ringing of an alarm clock. That's where a bucket can help. But first, you'll have to bear with me as I use some technical language to explain how this works.

When a noise is made (like the ringing of a bell for instance), some of those *sound wavy* things are created. If you make the noise *inside* a bucket, they bounce around like crazy in there. You see, sound waves, like bad dogs and my Uncle Roy (serving three to five), *hate* being confined, and when an opening is spotted they rush pell-mell for it.

To make practical use of this scientific stuff, you simply place an alarm clock way in the back of a five-gallon bucket and lay the bucket on its side with the opening near the ear of the sleeper. The actual *ringing* might not fully awaken them, but the racket the bucket and clock make when they roll off the night table, as the sleeper fumbles blindly to shut it off, *will!*

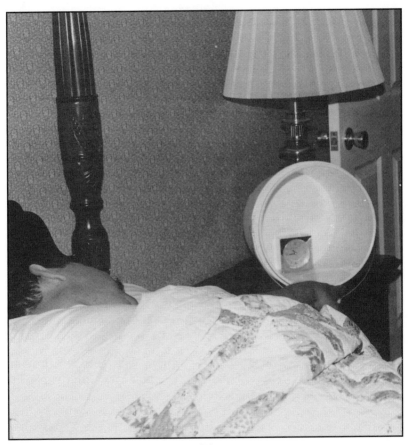

#86
THE NOT-A-SNOWBALL'S-CHANCE-IN-HELL BUCKET
Go on. Hit me with your best . . . uhhh!

You readers in the South might never have had the fun of romping in the snow—of sledding down an icy slope—or being hit, full in the face, with a ball of half-frozen *slush*.

The rest of you need to know how to make the ultimate snowball launcher.

1. Cut the bottom out of a bucket.
2. Attach a handle (like a drawer pull) to the bottom.
3. Drill four holes near the outer edges of the bottom and corresponding holes around the top of the bucket.
4. Attach strips of bicycle inner tube or surgical tubing between the bottom and top.

Now, position the "mortar" at the desired angle, load one or more snowballs into the "barrel" of your weapon, pull back with the handle, and fire! (Okay, these *are* meatballs, but it's *summer*.)

#87
THE PLATE-PACKIN'-MAMA BUCKET

Square pegs in round holes?

That's usually said about something you *shouldn't* try to do. But why is it, when we pack to move, we keep putting round things in square boxes? When it's time to pack the dinner plates, consider using a five-gallon bucket.

Stack one dish at a time with a layer of paper (or a foam plate) between. Cram all the dish towels and pot holders on top when the bucket is nearly full. With the lid secured, the round plates in the round bucket will move around very little. All the other kitchen utensils will fare as well when packed like this.

In fact, almost *anything* that will fit will travel better when packed in this nearly indestructible shipper. You might, in fact, consider this alternative the next time you plan to ship something valuable and *breakable* with one of those package-delivery companies.

Those delivery companies aren't *crazy* about the idea (they might charge you a few extra bucks), but they *will* accept something packaged like this. They can't damage the packaging and they're forced to handle it in an upright position.

#88

THE TIPTOE-THROUGH-THE-TULIPS BUCKET

Tiny Tim, we miss you.

Stepping stones are a nice touch in a flower garden or any pathway. And if you can't find your bucket boots, they'll keep the mud off your shoes. But why pay those big prices the home-supply stores charge for the premade kind when you can make them yourself?

1. Excavate a path where the stepping stones will be placed. You only need to make this about three inches deep.
2. Cut three inches off the bottoms of two buckets.
3. Mix up *half* a bag of concrete mix. (Have you made that cement mixer yet?)
4. Pour the concrete into the two bucket-bottom molds (each will hold about 290 cubic inches—about a quarter of a sack), and allow to set for about five minutes.
5. Flop the molds over into the excavated path where you want the "stones" to remain. Remove the bucket molds immediately and allow the concrete to dry for a day. Then you can fill in around them with soil or mulch.

#89
THE FIVE-GALLON-FORTRESS BUCKET

Good protection from snowball cannons.

When was the last time you went out and *played* in the snow? Sure, you shovel the driveway and walks and maybe you even ski, but don't you miss the fun you had as a youth?

Recapture that by building a snow fort. This is no namby-pamby child's construction, either. This is a manly or womanly construction with walls a *foot* thick!

You've got to wait for the right kind of snow, though—the slightly wet, sticky type. That fluffy, sissy *powder* you skiers like won't do. I'm talking *builder's* snow!

Scoop the snow into a five-gallon bucket by sweeping it across the surface. Then top it off with a few handfuls and pack it down slightly. Immediately upend the bucket at the chosen site. Build the walls by overlapping the joints.

NOTE: This is fun for a while, but unlike when you were a child, you will find that you get *tired*. That's when you tell the kids that the really *good* snow is in the driveway. Then go inside.

#90
THE BIGASS-BASS BUCKET
Maybe he *is* just a legend, but I'll find out.

There's a place down on the river that all the local fishermen talk about. There lurks the biggest, meanest largemouth bass ever seen. Almost everyone has hooked him at least once, but he just surfaces, shakes like a belly dancer, and spits the lure right back at whoever was foolish enough to try and land him. He has to be a remarkable fish, since every time someone has reported *nearly* catching him, his size has increased from the previous report.

Well, based on the last story I heard, I've built myself a lure that will finally, and at last, bring that lunker in. I'm not giving you this plan because that fish is *mine!*

#91
THE SHIVERING-SHOWER BUCKET
EEYOWWWW!

Traditionally, when just the men gather at some primitive camp, we are there to indulge our primal instincts: hunting, fishing, building fires, telling dirty jokes, drinking fermented grain beverages, and scratching *anywhere* we want to scratch. Since we seldom bathe at these testosterone-induced pilgrimages, we do a *lot* of scratching.

But women, children, and men who plan to rejoin society find bathing necessary. The facilities for this, however, are not always available at campsites. The five-gallon bucket shower solves that problem.

Just punch or drill a lot of small holes in the bottom of a bucket, and suspend it from a tree limb. Provide some means of access to the bucket, such as a stump to stand on, and have someone pour water into the bucket as you instruct.

If the water source is a cold mountain stream, it's a good idea to draw the water some hours *before* your bath, to allow it time to warm up to the ambient temperature.

NOTE: Make sure that the person you choose to pour the water is someone you trust, probably not the guy who you beat at poker last night. Do you have any idea how *cold* water is that comes directly from the beer cooler?

183

#92
THE ALL-AROUND-THE-MULBERRY-BUSH BUCKET
Stop plant abuse, NOW!

Plants have feelings too, don't they? Oh, who cares? My wife, on the other hand, feels pretty strongly about some of the tender little flowers she plants in various spots around the lawn, in her never-ending quest to create the perfect obstacle course for our riding mower.

Not long ago, shortly after I had finished mowing the lawn, *someone* crept into our yard under cover of darkness, somehow silently started our mower, and ran over my wife's newly planted peonies.

After that, I cut circles out of five-gallon buckets (you can get three of them, about three and a half inches wide, from each bucket) and pushed them into the ground, surrounding the surviving plants. You can leave them their natural color (easier to see) or paint them green or brown to blend in better. Boy, if my wife ever catches that mad plant butcher . . .

#93
THE CHEWTABACCA BUCKET
I wouldn't *use* the candy dish if we had a spittoon.

In Victorian times, our homes were equipped with charming accessories for most any occasion or usage. One of the more indispensable was the spittoon, or cuspidor.

I know that many of you are struggling to give up smoking. Fortunately, there are alternatives to this distasteful habit. You can replace it with the more genteel one of chewing tobacco or "dipping" snuff. The many flavors available today make it ideal for the ladies, too.

Once you've switched, though, you need to equip your house with at least one spittoon. While many people make the five-gallon bucket the receptacle of choice, there's one modification that will make it more closely resemble the original design.

Place the lid on a bucket, and with an *electric heat* gun (the type used for stripping paint) set on low, heat the lid carefully until it becomes a bit soft. Don't *ever* use an open-flame torch. Then, place a bowling ball in the center to deform it. When it cools, cut a hole in the center.

The sloping sides of the top will direct slightly off center expectorations toward the hole, keeping the cuspidor nice and neat. The five-gallon design means you only need empty it *semiannually,* a feature your spouse will *love!*

187

#94
THE LOOK-HE-CAN-CATCH-IT-IN-HIS-MOUTH BUCKET
Wow! So can his *dog.*

We can't name the toy because it's a trademark, but you know those colorful, saucer-shaped plastic toys that you can sail through the air with a flick of the wrist?

Well, it's entirely possible that you could find yourself stranded somewhere with nothing but a five-gallon bucket (with a lid), a bowling ball, and a heat gun. And, if you're like the rest of us, you could be struck by an urge to toss one of those disks around with a companion.

And, since you *are* like the rest of us, you'll remember the instructions for making a five-gallon spittoon, and how to deform a bucket lid into a concave object (it's *convex* when you turn it over, genius). This produces something that's considerably more aerodynamic than bucket lids normally are. Why? Because the air pressure is greater under the . . . wait a minute. You didn't buy this book to learn *physics,* did you?

If your companion happens to be a dog, you are *so* lucky. When this last happened to me, I was with a cat. While the cat seemed somewhat intrigued by the heating and forming process, it showed little interest in chasing and catching the object when thrown.

#95
THE I'M-SORRY-IT-AIN'T-SILVER BUCKET

May I serve you?

Many elegant homes, restaurants, and resorts have switched from using silver-plated trays for serving drinks and appetizers to using those made from the bottom one and a half inches of a five-gallon bucket. They're lightweight, nearly indestructible, catch small spills, and are easy to clean. They also cost *nothing*.

Seriously folks, they *do* make nice little trays for serving, especially for those meals out on the deck. Children love them for serving their own snacks, and if they use them to set their drinks on while watching TV, spills won't make it onto the carpet.

#96
THE I'M-SORRY-IT-AIN'T-CERAMIC BUCKET
May I [insert use here]?

Many elegant homes, restaurants, and resorts have switched from using ceramic trays for [catching overwatering runoff from houseplants] to using those made from the bottom one and a half inches of a five-gallon bucket. They're lightweight, nearly indestructible, catch small spills, and are easy to clean. They also cost *nothing*.

Seriously folks, they *do* make nice little trays for [placing under houseplants], especially for those [houseplants] out on the deck. Children love them for [placing under] their own [houseplants], and if they use them to set their [houseplants] on while watching TV, spills won't make it onto the carpet.

What are you *saying?* You think I just *copied* my last use? What do you *want* from me? Sure there're some similarities, but . . . hey, if you wanted *literature,* why ain't you reading Dostoyevsky?

#97
THE BOUNTIFUL-BIRDS BUCKET
We just received a preapproved credit card for the Martins.

Purple Martins live in almost every part of the United States. Many people try to encourage these birds to take up residence near their homes because of their insatiable appetite for insects. A single bird can eat as many as two thousand mosquitoes a day, while the average human at a cookout probably eats less than *half* that many.

Compartmented martin houses (they only live in *colonies*) are costly, though. Instead of buying, make one like this:

1. Measure and cut four half-inch boards, six inches wide and as long as the bucket's diameter near the bottom.
2. Cut half-inch notches halfway through the centers so they'll fit together forming X's.
3. Place the first X in the bottom of the bucket, place a cut-to-fit bucket lid on top of that, and then another X.
4. Cut two-and-an-eighth-inch holes to make openings into each compartment formed by the X's.
5. Remove everything, then add perches near each hole using a wood screw through the inside of the bucket and into the end of a dowel or half-inch twig.

Put everything back in, replace the lid, and hang your new martin apartment house (at least eight feet above the ground).

#98
THE I-CAN'T-HOLD-IT-
THAT-LONG BUCKET

I'm not taking a nap, I'm watering the tree.

When planting trees and shrubs, it's suggested that you fill the hole with water, allow that to soak in, and then set the tree in place. After refilling the hole, you're supposed to then *water* it thoroughly. Usually, when you try to do this, a lot of the loose soil you just replaced runs off with the water you're trying to add to it. You have to water *slowly*.

I'm not that patient. So usually I just laid the hose down near the tree, turned the water down to a trickle, and went off to do something else. The last time I did that, I forgot all about the running water until two days later, when my neighbor pointed out this strange area of wet ground in his lawn.

"Underground spring," I shouted, as I ran home through the spongy turf.

The next time I planted something, I used a five-gallon bucket. If you recall the timer we made earlier, you'll remember that a hole made with an 8d nail will allow five gallons of water to escape from a bucket over a period of a half hour. That's *just* the right amount of water *and* time for thoroughly saturating a newly planted tree.

Set the bucket near the base of the bush, fill it, then turn the water *off*.

#99
THE KIDDIE-ROOM-WALL BUCKET
Please Mom, let *me* put my clothes away.

You'll have to be a tiny bit more ambitious to tackle this one. It's not major renovation work, but it does require a little more effort and material than the rest of the projects in this book. The results are worth the effort, though.

1. Pick a wall in a child's room and fasten a one-by-two board to it six inches up from the floor and another board two feet up.
2. Using a bucket that's been sawed off right below the shoulder as a pattern, draw evenly spaced circles on a two-by-eight sheet of 3/4-inch plywood (a four-by-eight sheet ripped), and cut the openings out with a jigsaw. You need enough plywood to extend the length of the chosen wall.
3. Measure from the bottom of a bucket to the shoulder and fasten one-by-two boards to the floor at a distance three-quarters of an inch less than that measurement.
4. Fasten the plywood with holes to the floorboard.
5. Rest the other half of the ripped plywood on the top edge of the hole-cut plywood and the top wall board and fasten

everything together with finishing nails. Finish or paint the plywood as you choose.

6. Slide brightly painted, handleless buckets into the openings, with their bottoms supported by the lower wall boards.

The kids will like putting their clothing and toys away in the buckets, and using the two-foot-wide top as a shelf and desk.

#100
THE BETTER-SAVE-THOSE-PLASTIC-BAGS BUCKET

If they make it through the grocery store parking lot ...

. . . they can be put to use at home later on. At our house, we hate to throw them away. Who am I kidding. If you look in our refrigerator, you'll see that we hate to throw *anything* away.

In any case, when we *do* get around to cleaning out the refrigerator, or have some other sloppy garbage to wrap up (wait, I think I might *eat* that), we reach for one of those plastic grocery bags.

We tried saving them in paper bags and even inside *other* plastic bags. The best method of keeping them turned out to be a five-gallon bucket with a five-inch hole cut in the lid.

As you accumulate them, stuff them into the bucket and stir them around. Now when you need one, pull it up through the hole. Usually another will pop up like a tissue in a tissue box. You'll find *lots* of reuses for these bags, and if you think of enough, you can write a book. But, who would *read* such a stupid book?

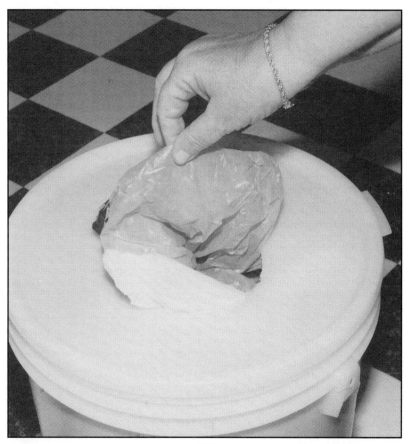

#101
THE WAAAY-UP-HIGH BUCKET
It don't mean a thing if it ain't got that swing.

A variation on the old-fashioned tire swing can be made in a few minutes from a five-gallon bucket. Just cut the last two inches off a sturdy bucket, drill a hole large enough to pass a strong rope through, find a large washer, and you're halfway there.

Invert the partial bucket so the cut edges point down, push the rope through the hole and the center of the washer, and tie a large knot or two in the end of the rope. Next just find a suitable tree limb to hang the bucket swing from. Now, "Push me. Push me!"

#102
THE IS-THIS-BIG-ENOUGH?
ICED-TEA BUCKET

How 'bout another glassa that, huh?

Are you *refreshed* yet? What *is* it with these huge iced tea glasses. I like iced tea, but the glasses just seem to be getting larger and larger. Every time my wife sees a new set of glasses designed for this purpose, she buys them.

"I know we have some," she says. "But these will hold so much *more*." They sure will. Just looking at them makes me need to pee.

Well, once more, I'm indulging her by *making* her something she really wants.

Oh, you wanted that *un*sweetened?

#103
THE SIGN-OF-THE-TIMES BUCKET

Keep out! Private drive!
Go away! We're not home!

That's just a *few* of the signs my neighbors drag out of their garages when they see me coming. They're so proud of their handiwork that they just have to show it off to me. After all, I'm the one who showed them how easy it is to make a portable sign in the first place, not to mention *bucket boots* and *alpenhorns*. How could they *not* be grateful?

If *you* have need of a sign that will only be displayed on occasion, a five-gallon bucket makes the perfect stand to support it. Fill a bucket with a single bag of mixed concrete and insert your signpost (mailbox, badminton, volleyball posts, etc.). When set, it'll weigh about eighty pounds, so it's not going to blow over. But if you leave the handle attached you can easily move them as needed.

That's an interesting sign my neighbor Marlene is putting up right now. Let's see, it says, "This is *not* the house where the NUT lives. Do NOT drop five-gallon buckets off here!"

207

#104
THE FLY-ME-TO-THE-MOON BUCKET
A sucker born every minute.

Some people are *so* gullible. Just the other day, I met a guy who was trying to sell this entire bucket full of rocks brought back from the moon. He told me that he was an astronaut, and that this rare *square* bucket, designed by NASA, was a gift from the space program when he retired. He hated to part with it and the moon rocks, but his wife told him to clean out the basement or else! I can sympathize with him *there*.

Anyway, although I hated taking advantage of a national hero, I offered him *half* what he originally asked. The poor fool actually accepted my offer. Well, it's not *my* fault that some people are so easily bamboozled.

209

#105

THE INCREDIBLY FRAGILE EGO OF SVEN THE CURSING JUGGLER

Ahh #%!!@**&! I dropped the &%#2!* thing AGAIN!

As much as I hate doing this, I must end on a sad note. You've learned a lot of things you can do with a five-gallon bucket, and undoubtedly, you'll think of more. But lest you think this book is a license to try *anything,* I offer this cautionary tale of something you *can't* do with a bucket.

A few months ago, we were invited across the street to attend a birthday party for our neighbors' ten-year-old. For a special treat, they had hired Sven, "the man who juggles anything!" And he *was* impressive as he manipulated everything we could come up with.

He easily juggled dishes, chairs, fruit, bricks, and a caged bird. He juggled them in any combination while balancing awkward objects on his chin. The children, as well as the adults, were in *awe.* As he called for more and more bizarre items, we eagerly kept them coming; books, cans of sardines (in mustard *and* in oil), table lamps, and a freeze-dried squirrel mounted in a realistic pose. The man was an absolute *marvel.*

In the midst of this, I was struck by an *inspiration.* Quickly, I ran home and returned with three five-gallon buckets. When he saw what I was bringing, his jaw dropped. It literally *dropped!* I had never seen that

happen before. I thought it was an expression like "If looks could kill." That's when he shot me one of *those!*

He tried to juggle them. He *really* tried. But the handles flailed his face and struck him in the eyes. They wrapped around his elbows and pivoted, coming up *forcefully,* and no doubt *painfully,* under his chin, dislodging what I later learned was a *permanent* bridge. This was his worst nightmare, the one item he constantly hoped no one would think to challenge him with.

It was then that we learned that, although Sven earned his living entertaining children, he had a really *bad* temper. While the children listened with rapt attention, he regaled us with the vilest string of curses we had ever heard. He taught the kids things that they would say the rest of their lives when faced with *impossible* tasks.

He called the buckets things that you would think could only apply to mythical, dung-eating beasts. He called me *worse.* And, though I tried desperately to suppress it, I *laughed.*

My sniggering did absolutely *nothing* to improve Sven's disposition. He soon ran out of ordinary expletives, and began *inventing* words. That was too much. I had to leave. As I staggered across the street, convulsed with laughter, tears streaming down my face, I heard a five-gallon bucket clatter to the ground a few feet behind me.

BRINGIN' IN THE BUCKETS
Where do I GET me some of them things?

Now that you've read this informative book, you will, without doubt, find that you are experiencing an urgent need to acquire buckets. To lessen frustration, and prevent widespread rioting, this handy reference suggests several sources.

Food-service establishments—Restaurants, delicatessens, bakeries, and grocery stores (as well as some smaller specialty markets).

Contractors—Drywall, painting, and general contractors have them coming out of their . . . uh, vans.

Farm- and home-supply stores—Any establishment that sells things like seeds, nuts, bolts, and chain in "bulk."

Buy stuff in them—If you or someone you know belongs to one of those wholesale warehouse members-only buyers' clubs, you can get things like birdseed and laundry detergent by the bucket.

Find them—Strewn along the back roads of America, along with old tires and fast-food containers, buckets can be found where they were discarded by the unknowing. Inexplicably, they even wash ashore, like the shells of strange mollusks, where they can be harvested from the beaches.